# SCHÖNE LEUTE

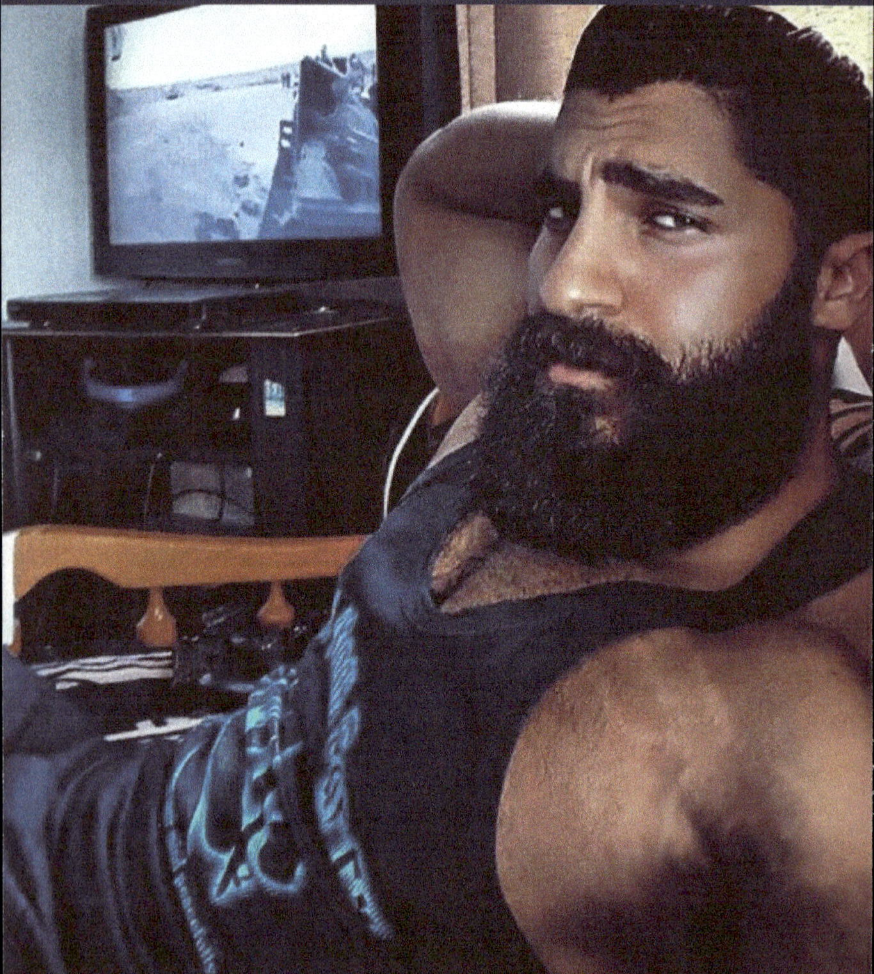

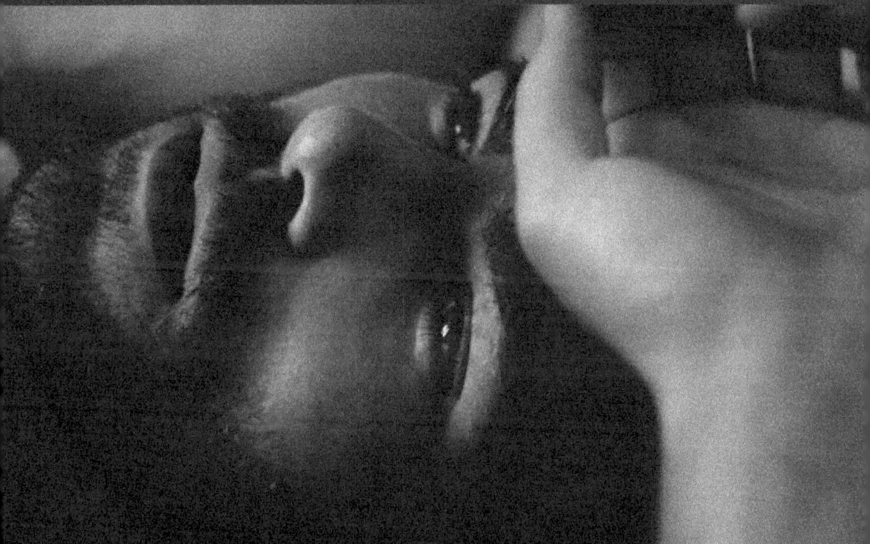

A|X

I'm
smalle
than
the othe

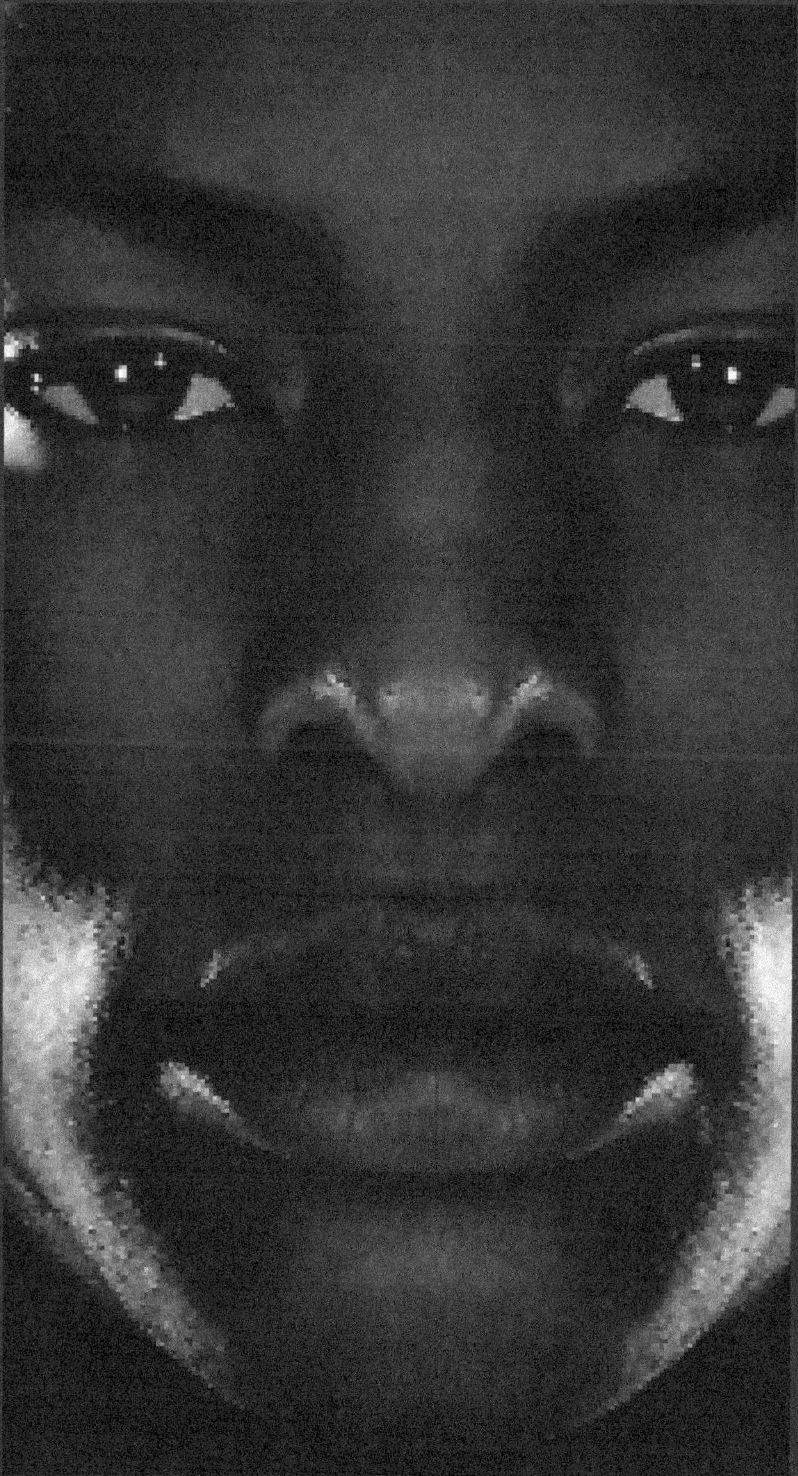

PEUGE

RealWorkoutsInc.co

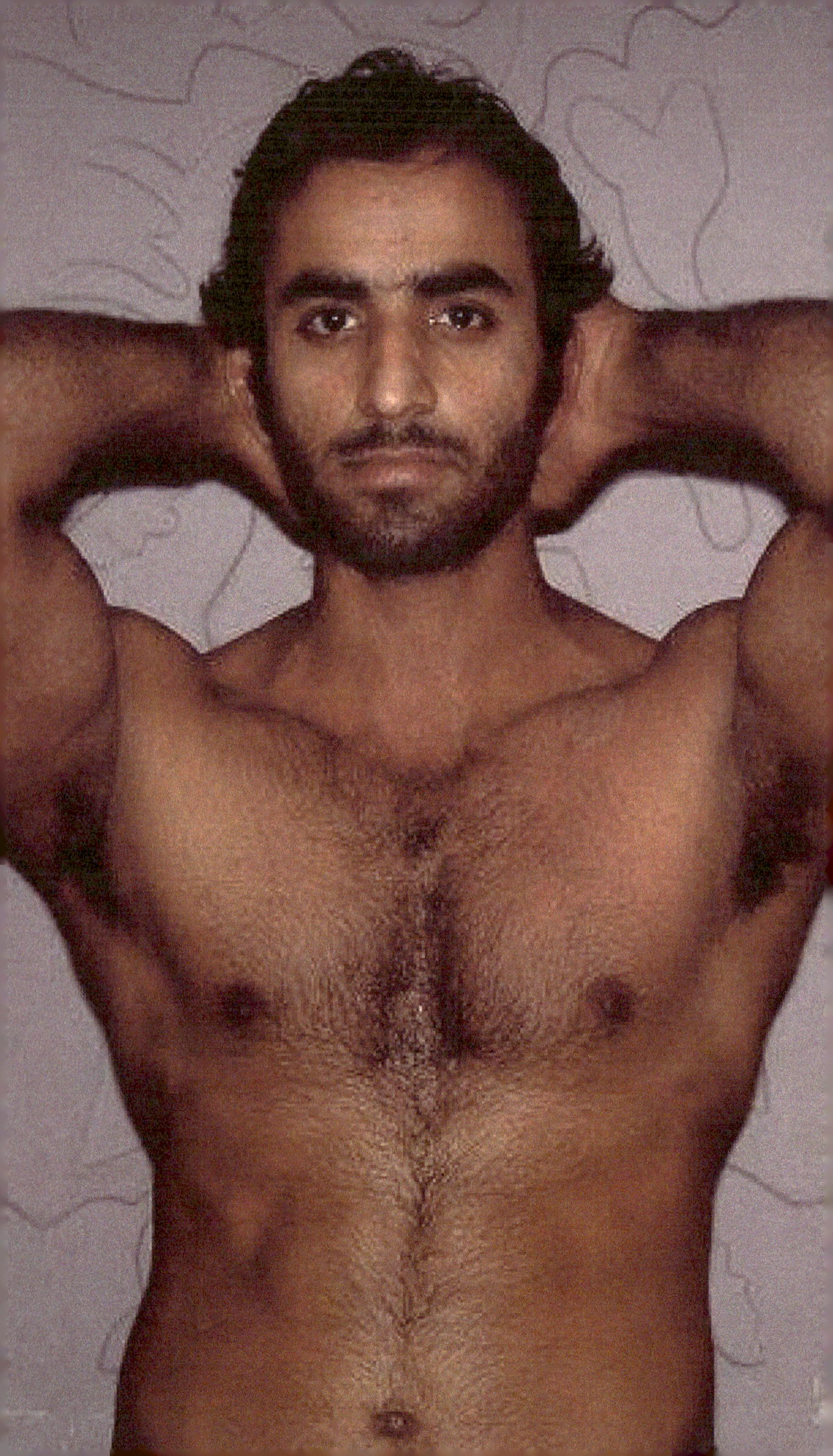

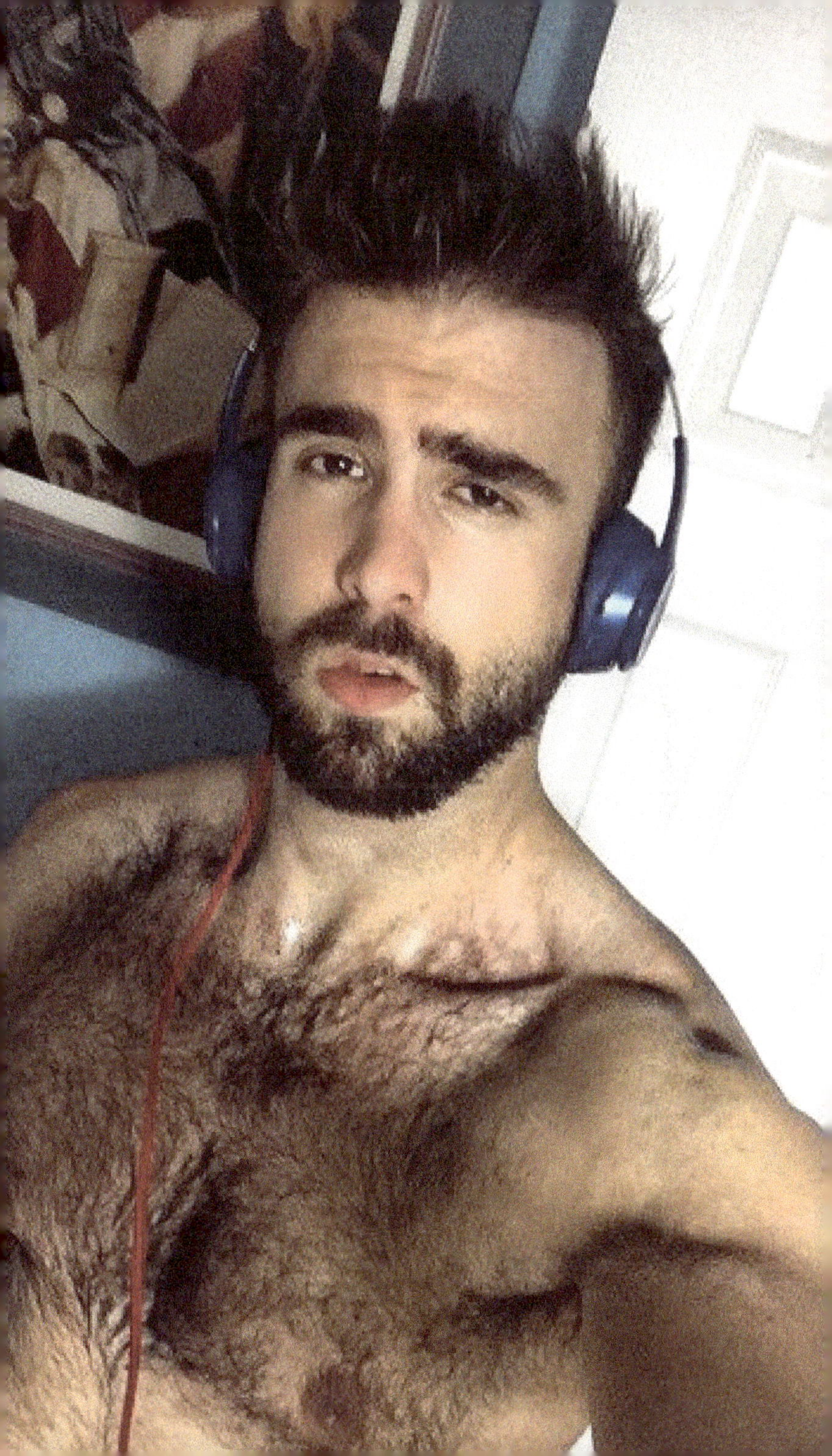

Diaph

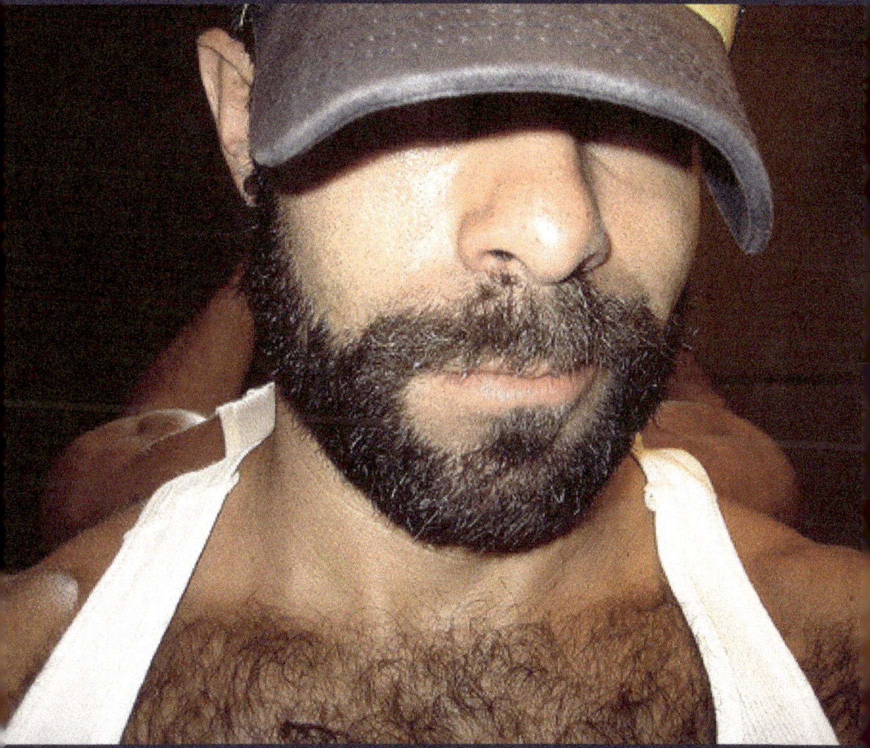

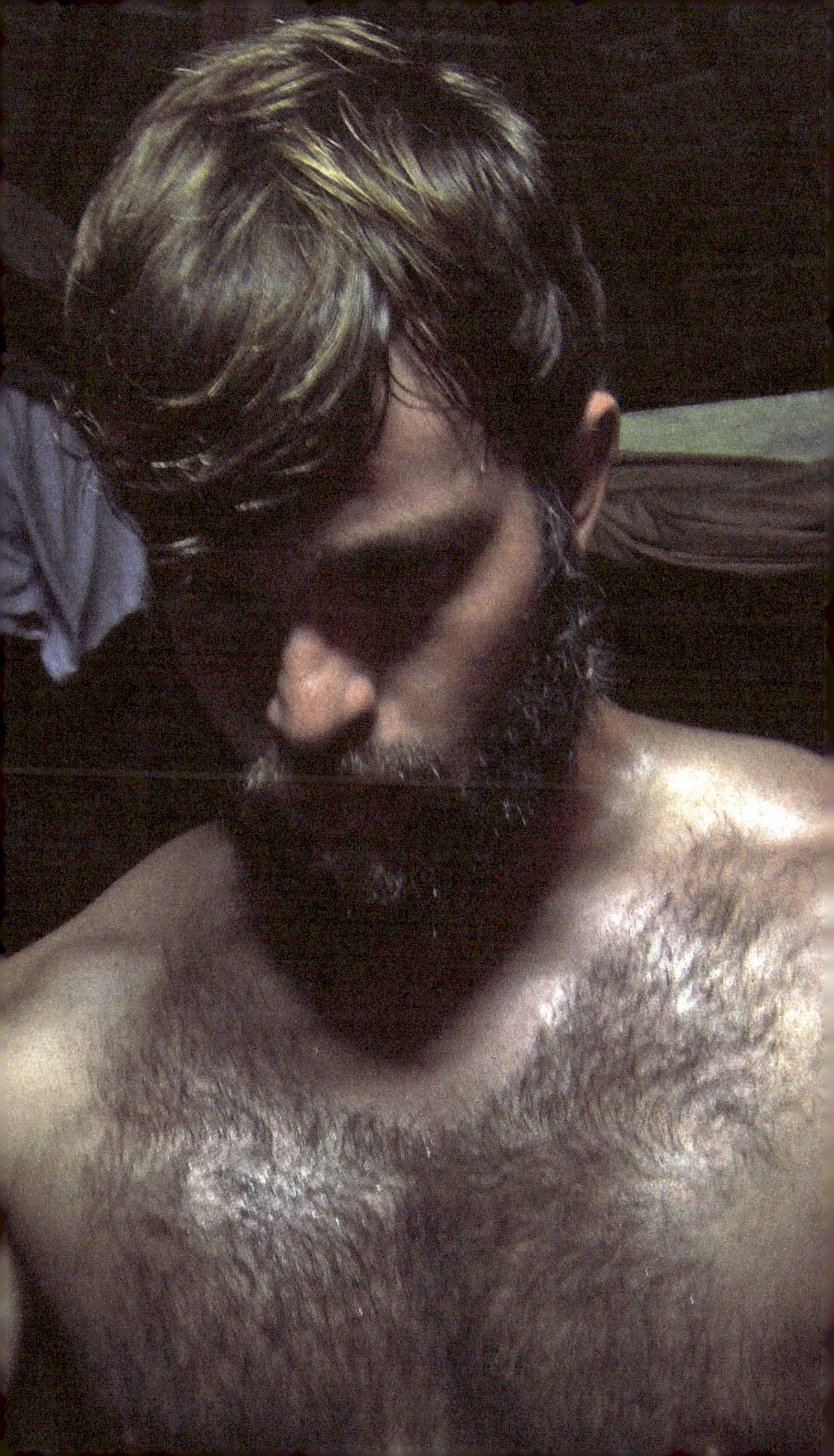

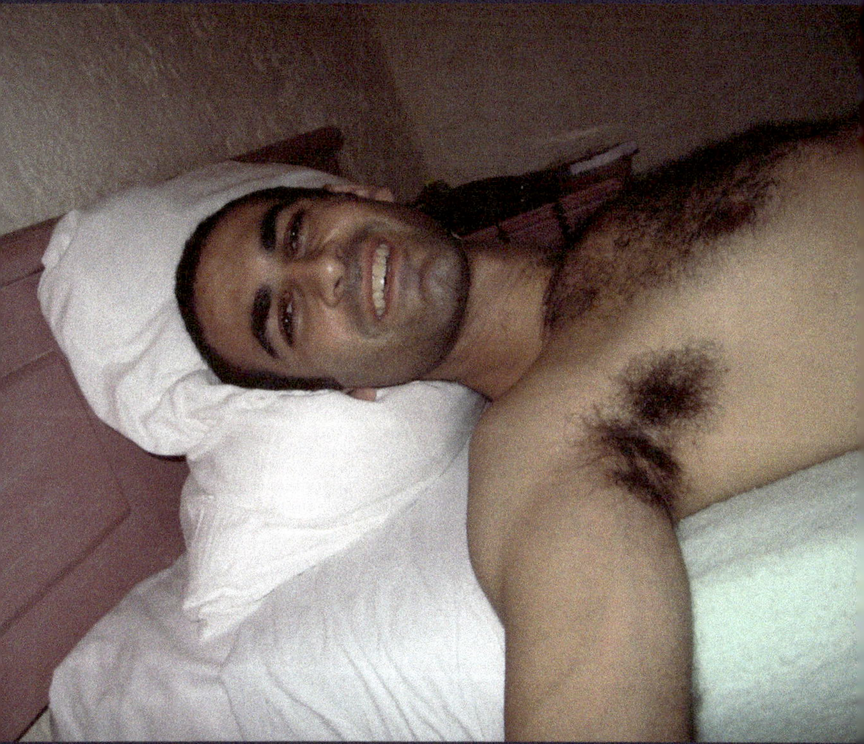

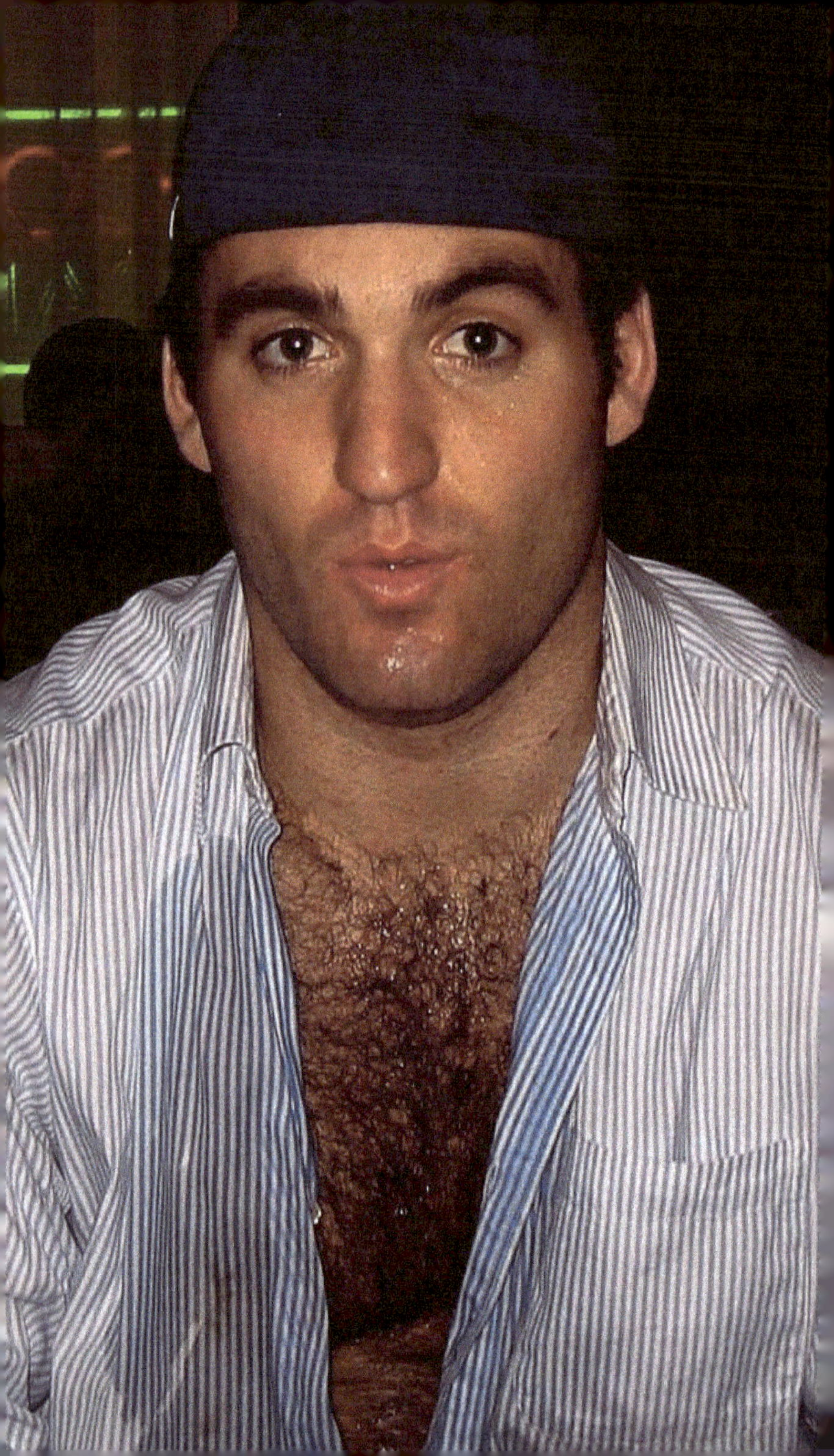

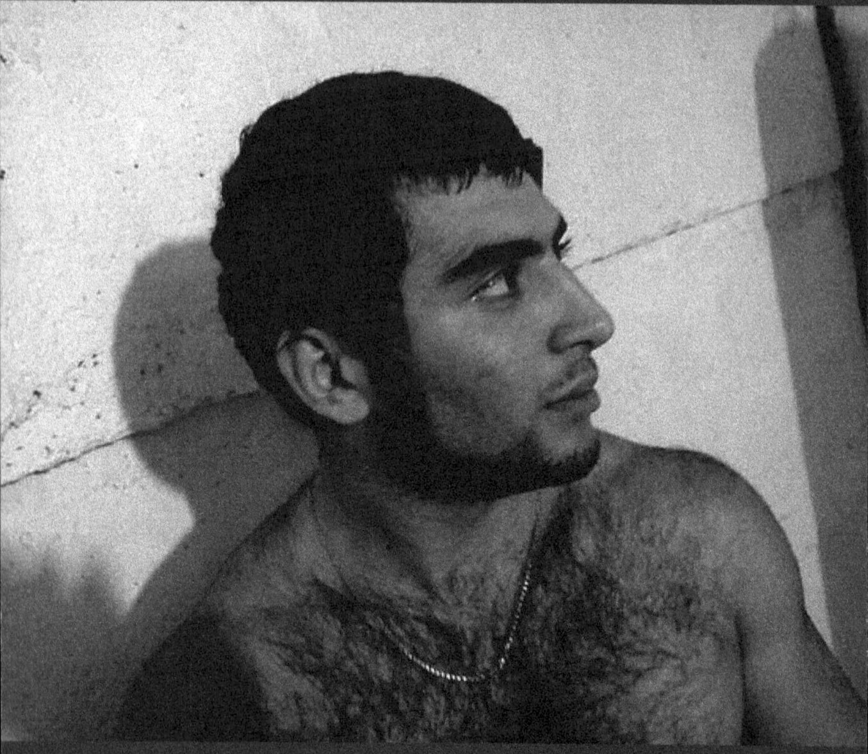

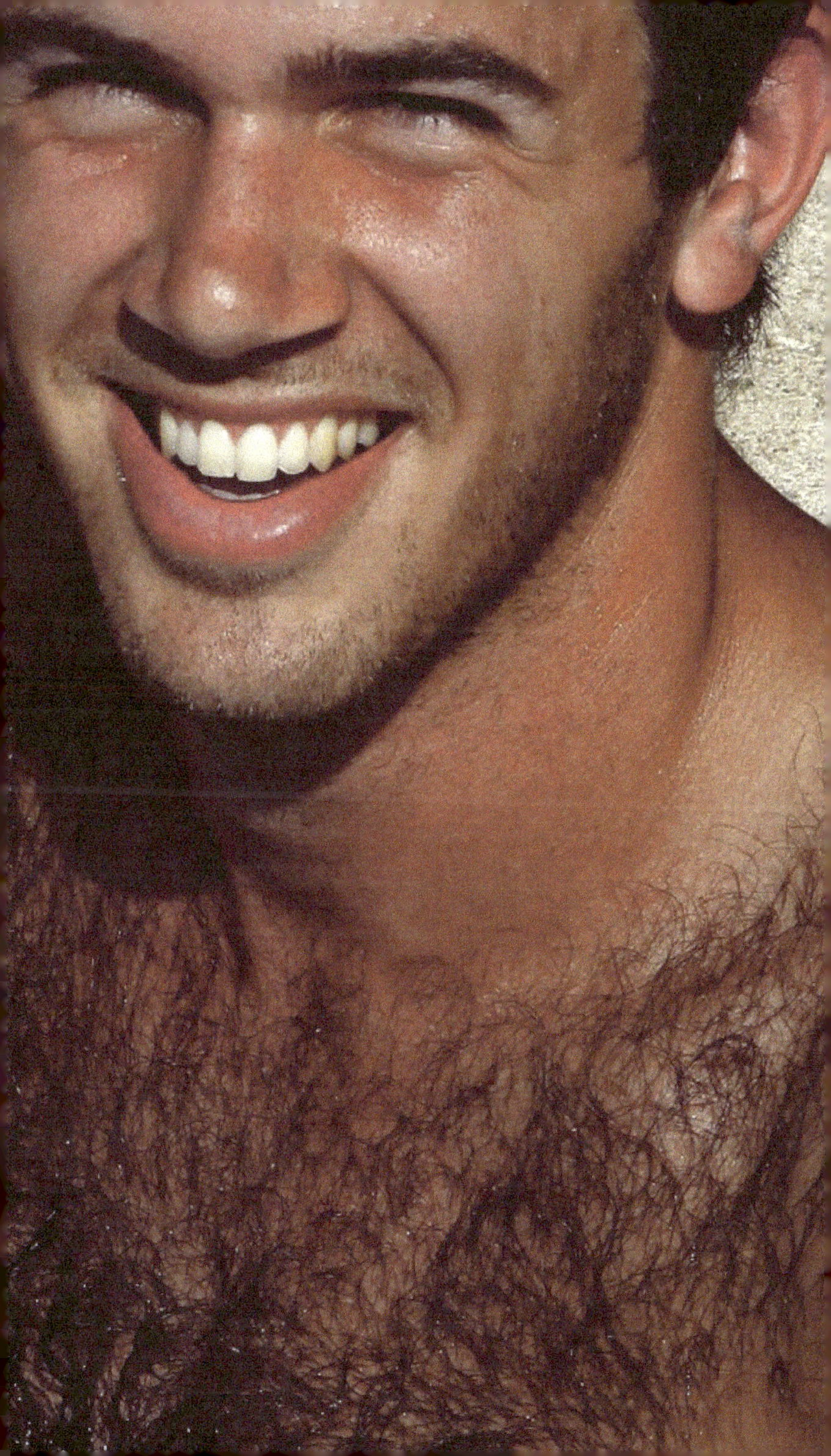

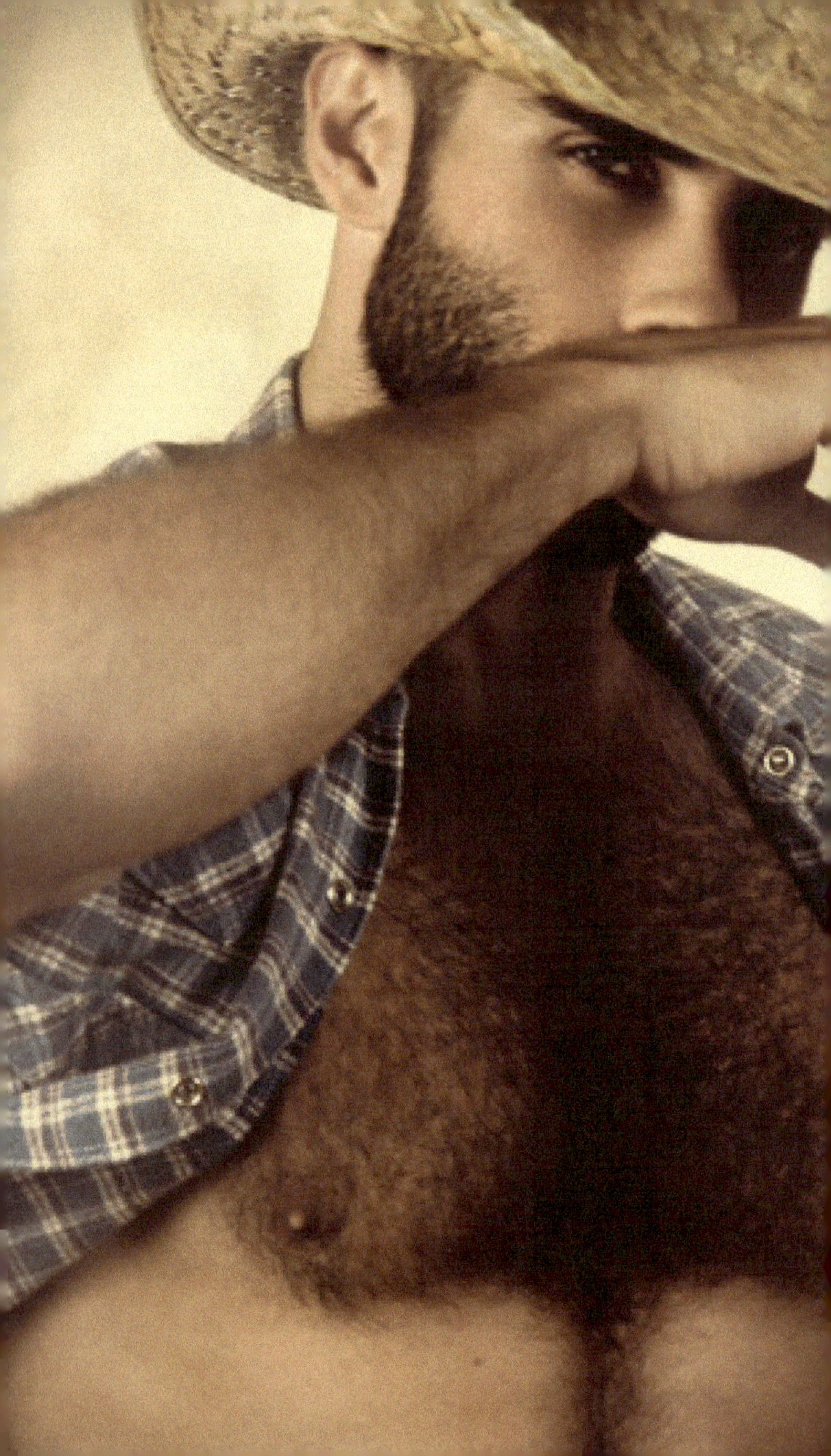

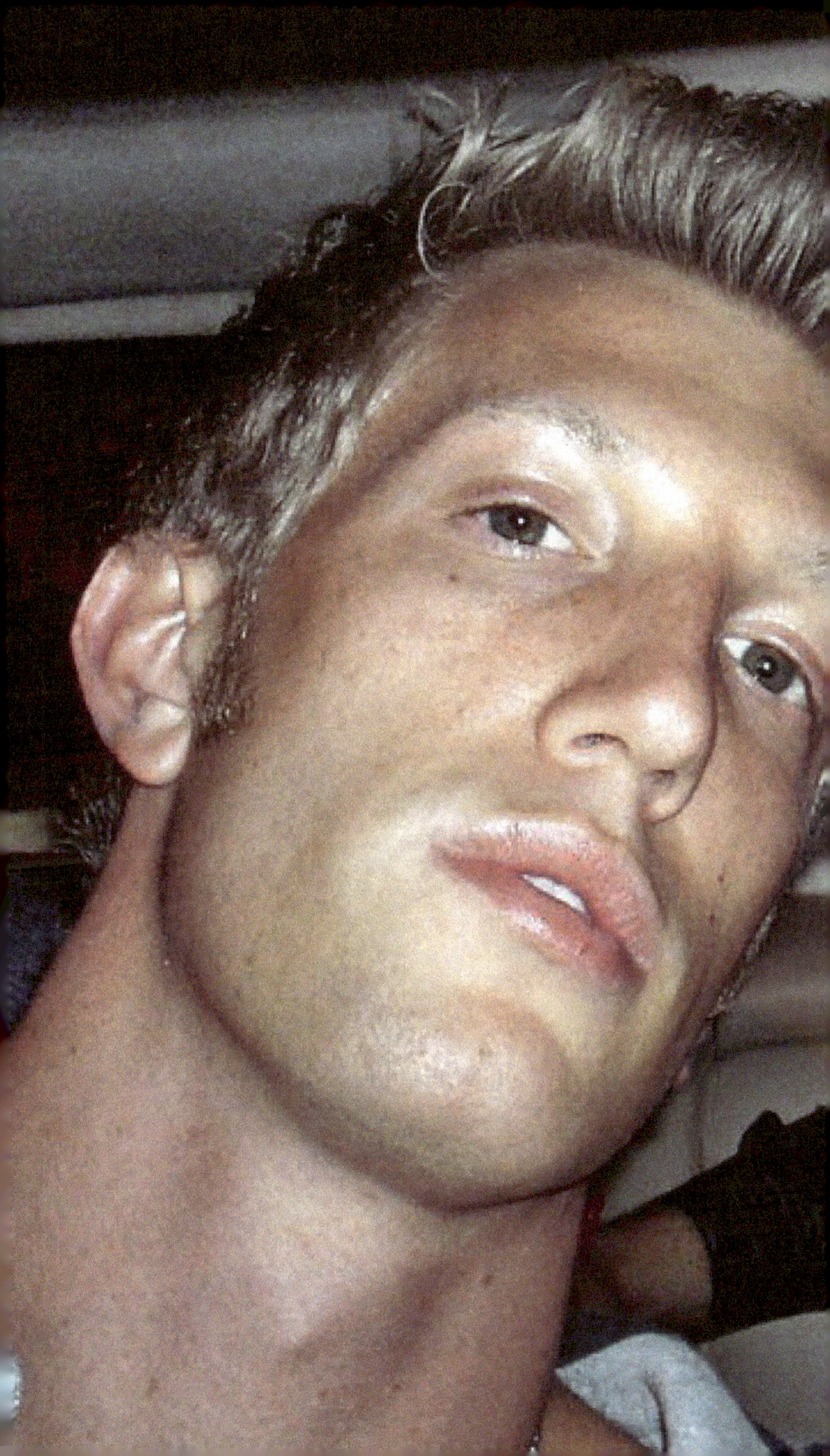

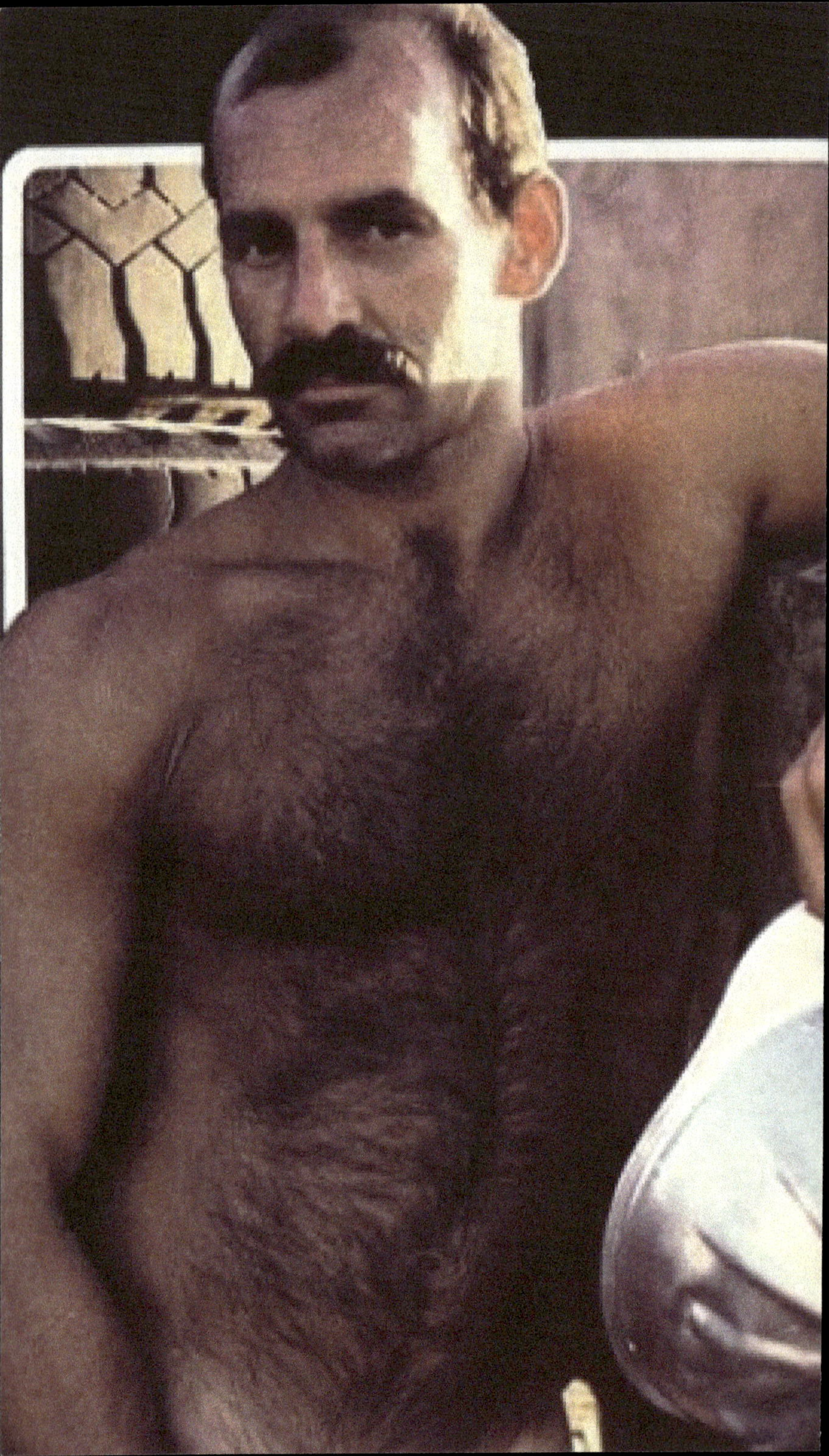

CPSIA information can be obtained
at www.ICGtesting.com
Printed in the USA
BVHW020055220519
548917BV00019BA/294/P

9 780368 769016